My Mahabharata

STORY, ACTIVITY & LIFE LESSONS

18+ Puzzles
& a Quiz

www.itihasika.com

INDIA · SINGAPORE · MALAYSIA

ISBN 979-8-89724-926-8

Mahabharata
The Story

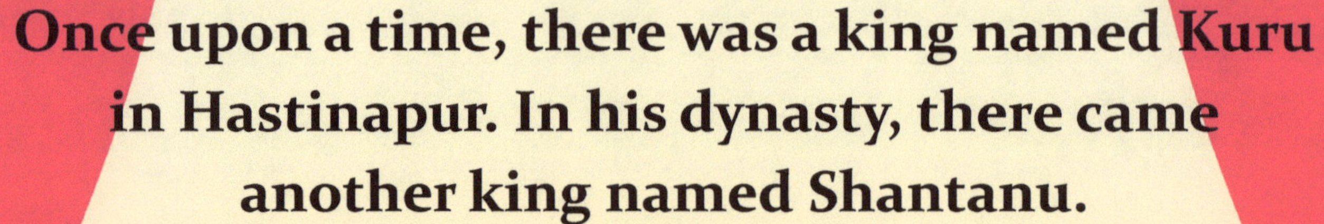

Once upon a time, there was a king named Kuru in Hastinapur. In his dynasty, there came another king named Shantanu.

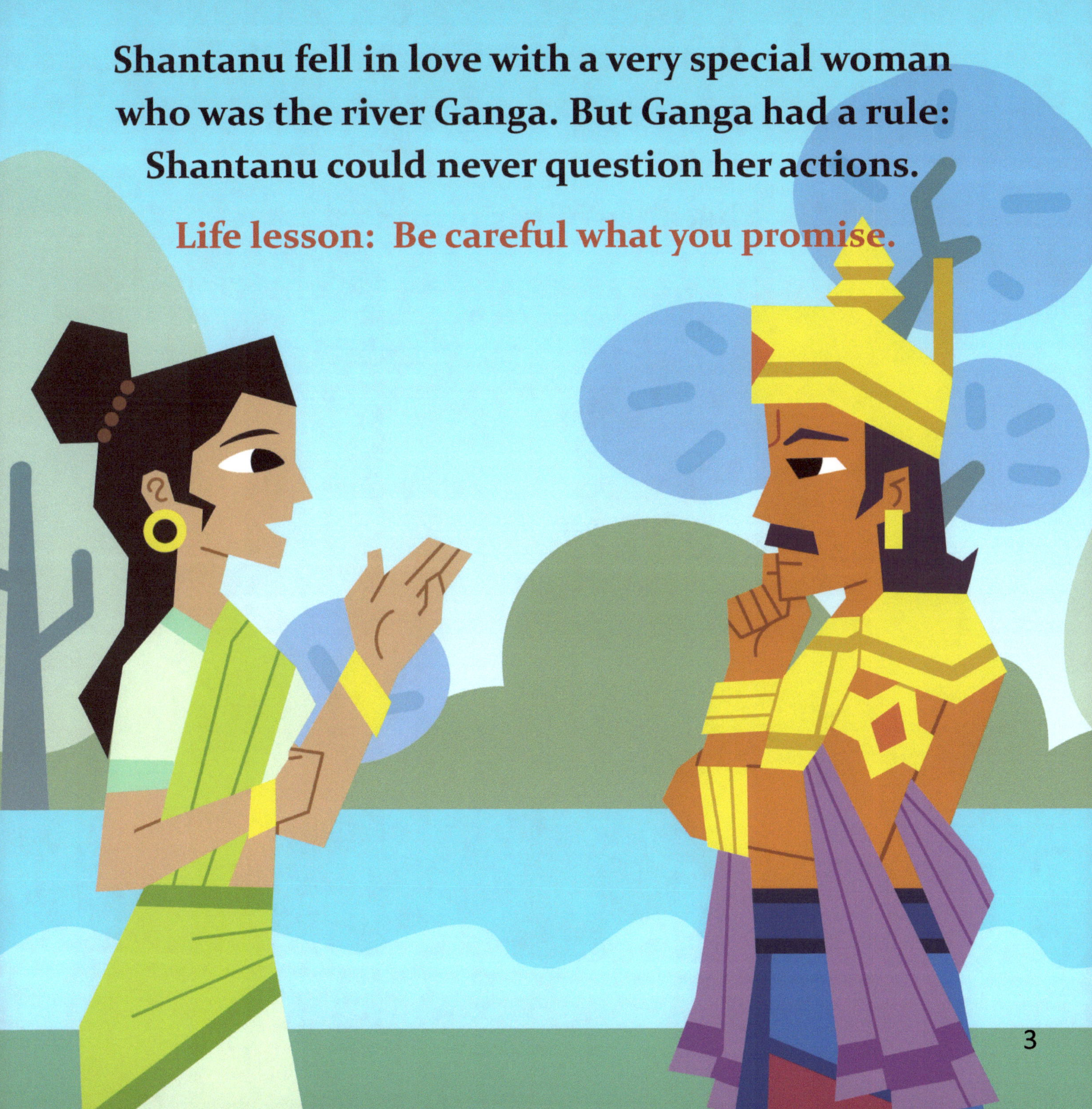

Shantanu fell in love with a very special woman who was the river Ganga. But Ganga had a rule: Shantanu could never question her actions.

Life lesson: Be careful what you promise.

They had seven children, but sadly,
Ganga drowned all the babies in the river!
Shantanu was shocked, but couldn't question her
because of his promise.

Shantanu stopped Ganga from drowning their eighth baby - Devavrata. Ganga explained that the babies were Gods, meant to return to heaven.
But she left him, as he broke his promise.

5

Shantanu was very sad. But when Devavrata grew up,
Ganga gave him to Shantanu.
Shantanu raised him, planning to make him king of
Hastinapur one day.

One day, Shantanu met another woman named Satyavati. He wanted to marry her, but her father had a condition. He said only Satyavati's children could be kings.

Shantanu disagreed. So prince Devavrata took a vow that he would never marry and have children. He was called 'Bhishma' after this.

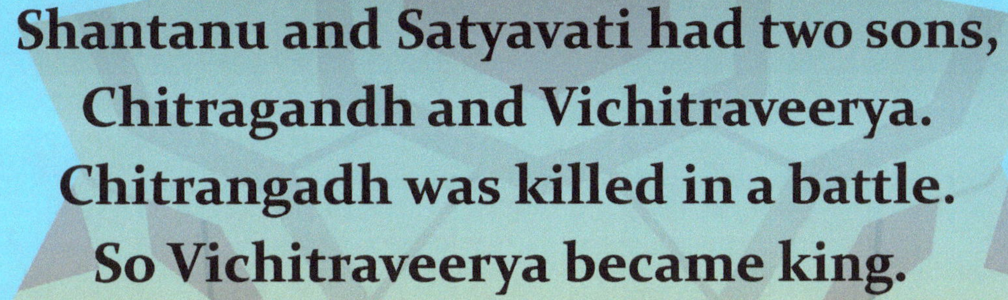

Shantanu and Satyavati had two sons,
Chitragandh and Vichitraveerya.
Chitrangadh was killed in a battle.
So Vichitraveerya became king.

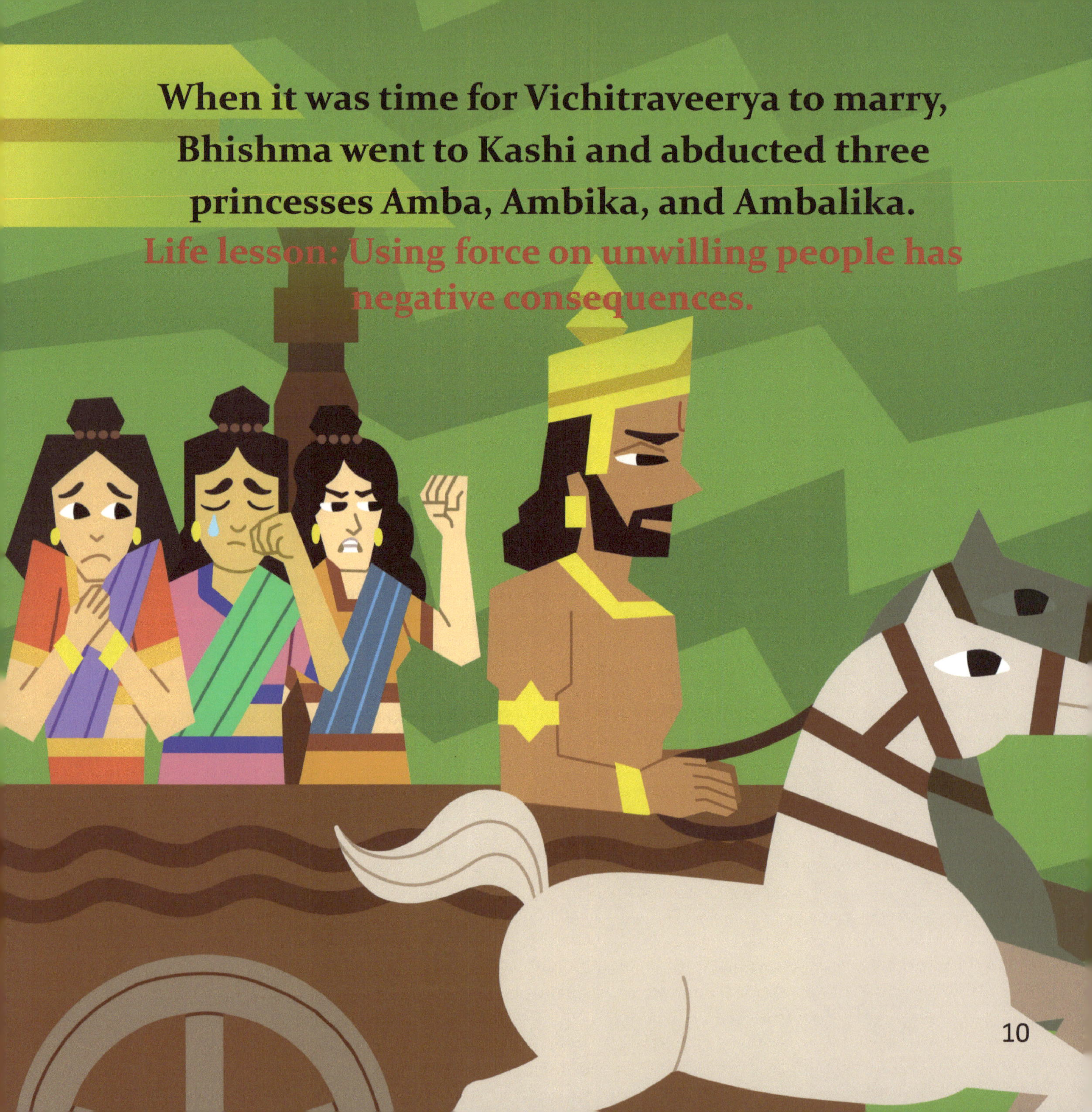

When it was time for Vichitraveerya to marry, Bhishma went to Kashi and abducted three princesses Amba, Ambika, and Ambalika.
Life lesson: Using force on unwilling people has negative consequences.

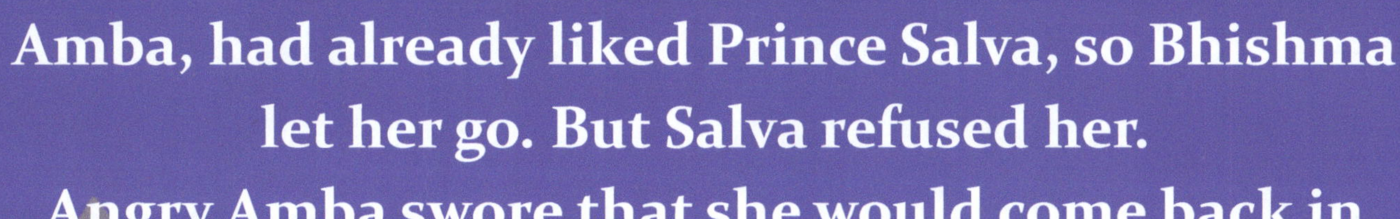

Amba, had already liked Prince Salva, so Bhishma
let her go. But Salva refused her.
Angry Amba swore that she would come back in
another life to cause Bhishma's death.

Vichitraveerya died without having any kids with his wives Ambalika or Ambika.
To get babies Satyavati called her son Rishi Vyasa who had magical powers.

When Ambika looked at ugly Vyasa she closed her eyes in horror. So her baby Dhritharashtra was born blind. When Ambalika looks at Vyasa she shivered with fear so her baby Pandu was born sickly.

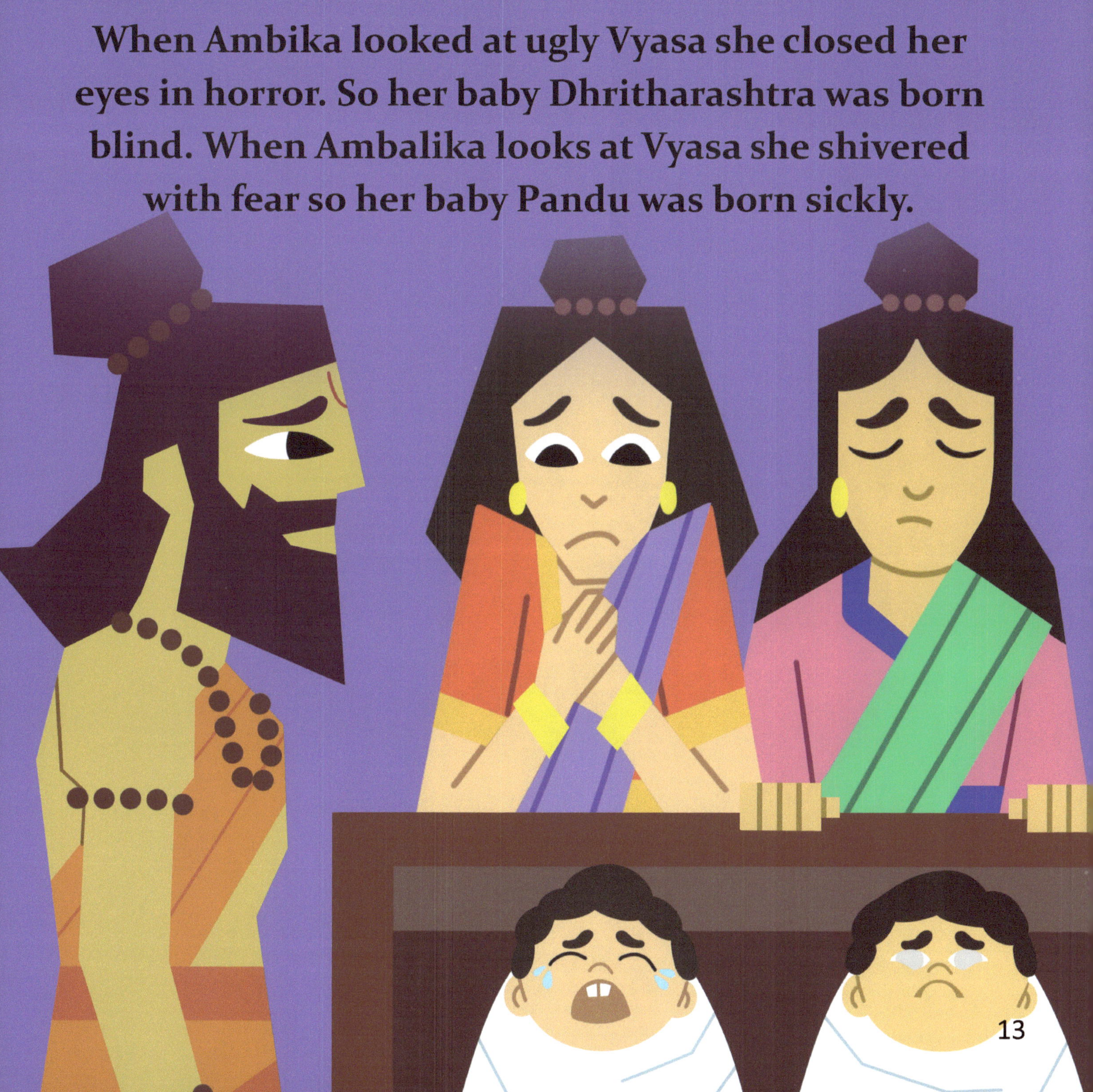

When Dhritharashtra grew up Bhishma married him to Princess Gandhari. Because Dhritharashtra was blind she put on a blindfold and swore never to use her eyes all her life.

This injustice made her brother Shakuni angry. He promised that one day he will destroy Hastinapur.

Life lesson: Who you marry can change your life.

Prince Pandu married a Princess called Kunti in a swayamvar. Later he also married Princess Madri to expand the empire.

When the time to nominate the king came,
though Dhritharashtra was older, Pandu was
made king as Dhritarashtra was blind.
This made Dhritarashtra very upset.
Life lesson: Merit is more important than seniority.

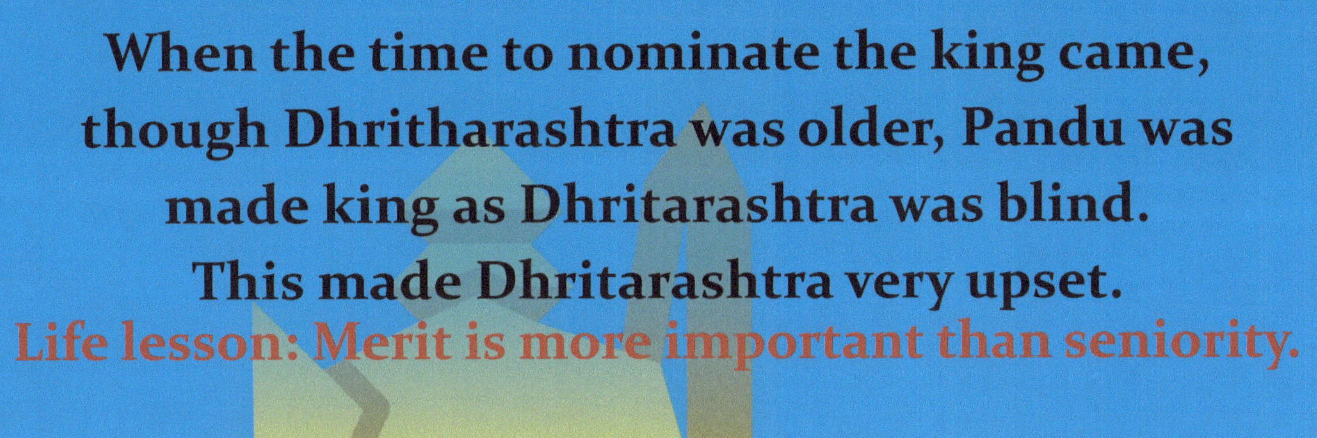

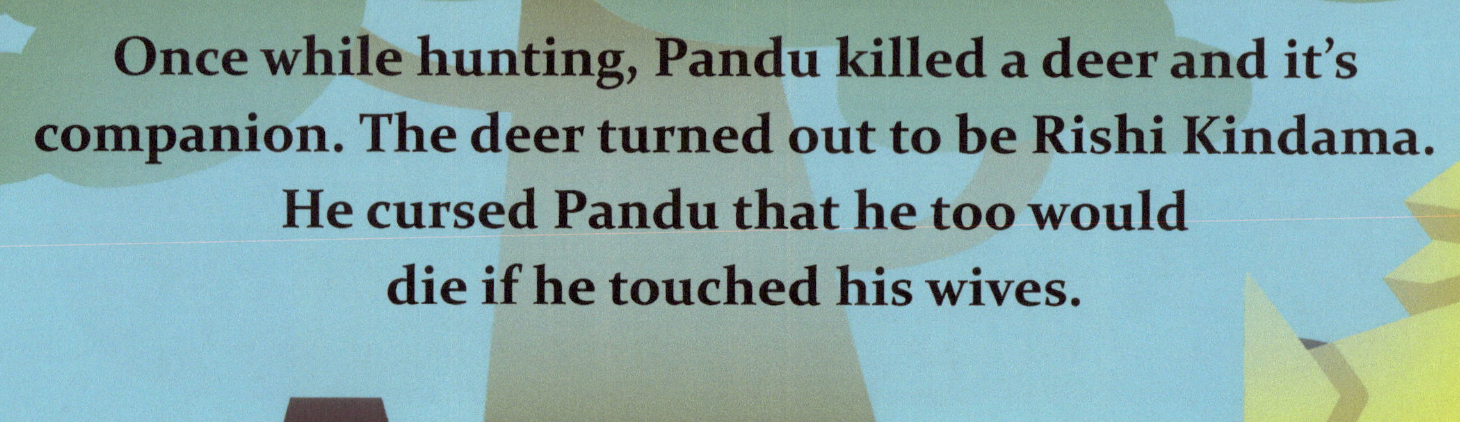

Once while hunting, Pandu killed a deer and it's companion. The deer turned out to be Rishi Kindama. He cursed Pandu that he too would die if he touched his wives.

Pandu left his kingdom and went to the forest
with his two wives to repent for his sin.
Dhritarashtra became the king.

19

Kunti revealed a secret that she knew a spell by which she can summon Gods and create children. Pandu asked her to use the spell for children to inherit the kingdom.

Kunti got Yudhishthira with Yam dev, Bhima from
Vayu dev and Arjuna from Indra dev.
Madri got Nakul and Sahadev from Ashwini
Kumars. The five brothers were called Pandavas.

21

But Kunti had one more secret. Long ago, she had accidentally used this spell and had a child called Karna with the Sun God. Scared, she abandoned the baby in a river.

Baby Karna was found by charioteer Adhiratha
and his wife Radha. They had no children and
decide to raise him. Unfortunately growing up he
got three curses.

23

The first curse was from mother earth.
He had squeezed her to get back milk that a child
had spilt. She cursed him that during battle his
wheel would get stuck in mud.

24

The second curse was when he accidentally killed a Brahmin's cow. The Brahmin cursed him that he'll be killed in battle when he's helpless.

25

The third was from guru Parshuram who had sworn to never train Kshatriyas. He thought Karna lied about not being Kshatriya and cursed him to forget mantras when he needs them.

Gandhari was upset that Kunti had kids and she didn't. Vyasa took a lump of her flesh and put it in 100 pots from which Kaurava babies were born. Duryodhana was the eldest.

Once Pandu touched his wife Madri and died
because of the curse. So Kunti took the Pandavas
back to Hastinapur Kingdom.
Bhishma got Kripacharya & Dronacharya as gurus.

28

Drona had a friend named Drupad, who had
insulted him after becoming king.
So Drona agreed to train the princes and asked
them to capture Drupad as his fee upon
completing the training.

Duryodhana, the eldest Kaurava was a wicked person who was always searching for a way to kill the Pandavas. He was insecure that the throne of Hastinapur will be taken from him.

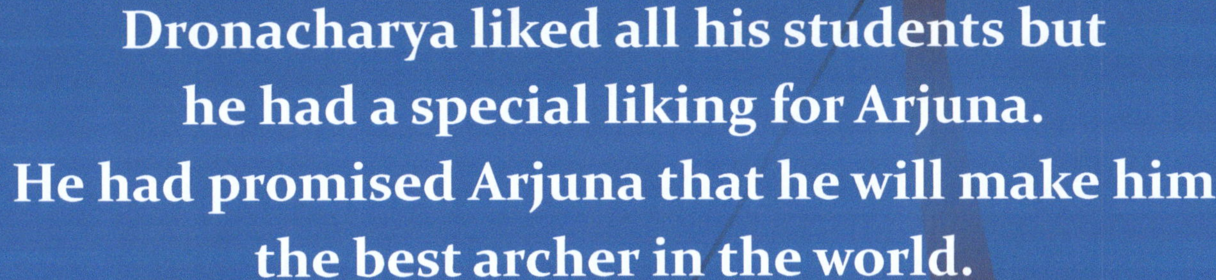

Dronacharya liked all his students but
he had a special liking for Arjuna.
He had promised Arjuna that he will make him
the best archer in the world.

Drona saw a boy, Ekalavya, shooting arrows into a
dog's mouth without harming it.
Ekalavya had learned archery from
Drona's statue. Fearing he'd surpass Arjuna,
Drona demanded Ekalavya's thumb as fee.

Life lesson: The penalty for stealing knowledge is heavy.

Finally the day came for the princes to show their skill. A stranger appeared, claiming to be better than Arjuna. This was Karna, Kunti's eldest secret son.

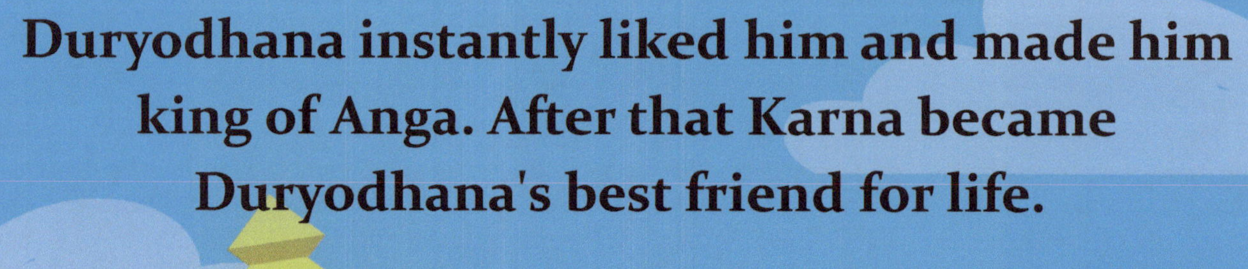

Duryodhana instantly liked him and made him king of Anga. After that Karna became Duryodhana's best friend for life.

Dhritharashtra was forced to declare Yudhishthira as crown Prince. So Duryodhana and his evil uncle Shakuni built a house made of wax called 'Lakshagrah' where they'd burn and kill Pandavas.

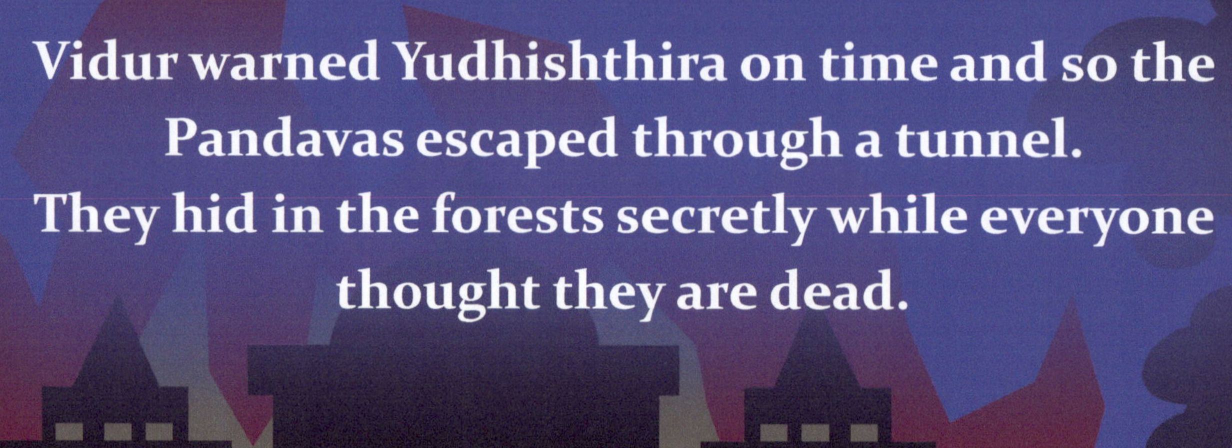

Vidur warned Yudhishthira on time and so the
Pandavas escaped through a tunnel.
They hid in the forests secretly while everyone
thought they are dead.

In the forest, Bhima married a demoness called
Hidimba, and they had a son called Ghatotkach.
Arjuna found out that a beautiful princess,
Draupadi, was planning on getting married.

Draupadi placed a condition on anyone who wanted to marry her. They had to be a great archer who could shoot an arrow into a fish's eye while looking into its reflection in the water. Arjuna did it and married Draupadi.

When the Pandavas brought Draupadi home, they
told Kunti they had a surprise.
Without looking, Kunti said to share it.
Bound by her word, Draupadi became the wife of
all five Pandavas.

Life lesson: Be careful of what you speak.

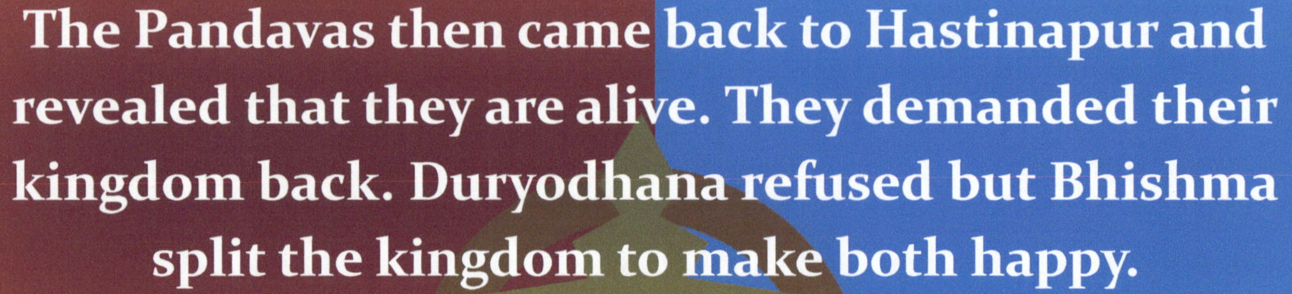

The Pandavas then came back to Hastinapur and revealed that they are alive. They demanded their kingdom back. Duryodhana refused but Bhishma split the kingdom to make both happy.

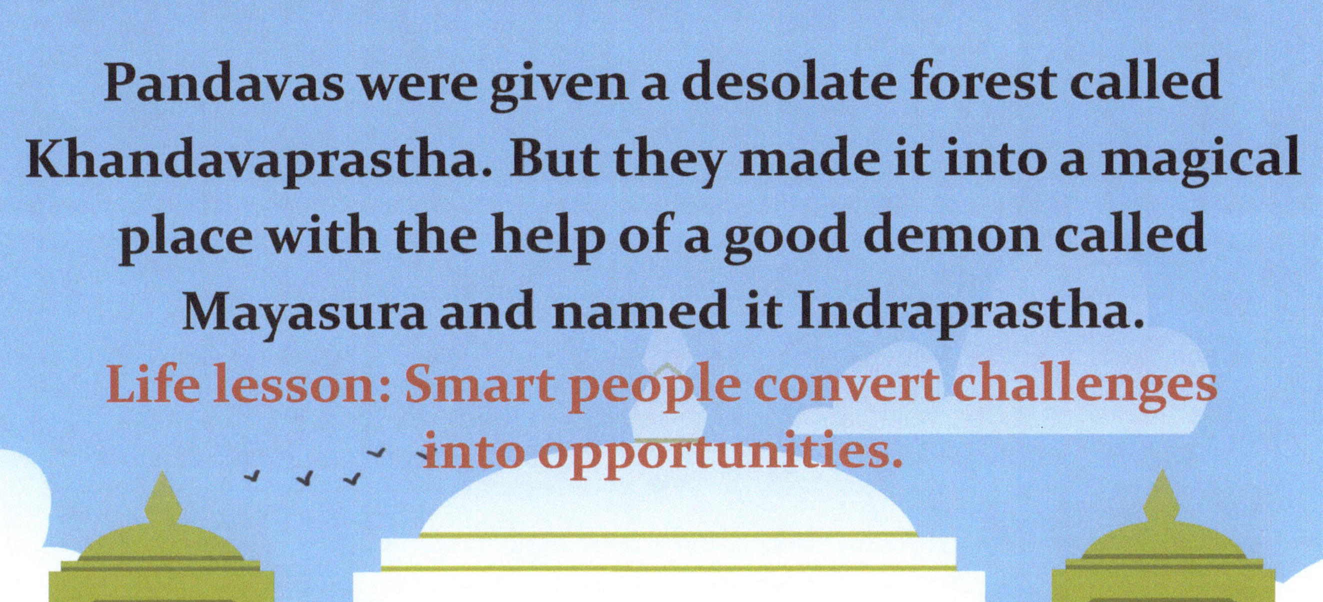

Pandavas were given a desolate forest called Khandavaprastha. But they made it into a magical place with the help of a good demon called Mayasura and named it Indraprastha.

Life lesson: Smart people convert challenges into opportunities.

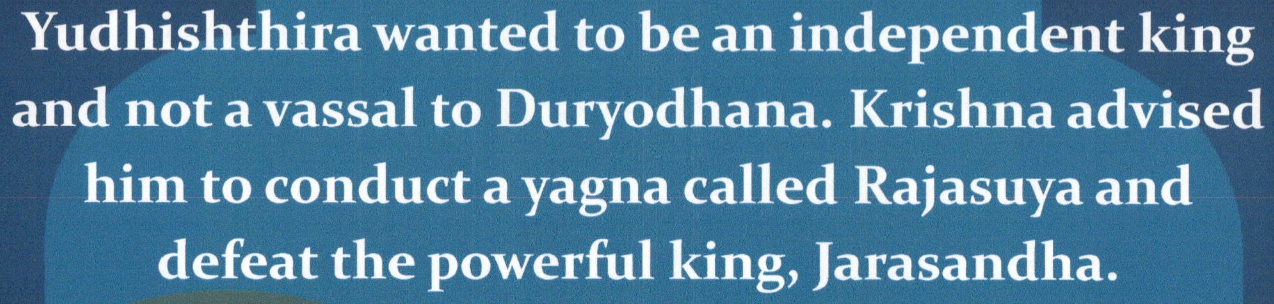

Yudhishthira wanted to be an independent king and not a vassal to Duryodhana. Krishna advised him to conduct a yagna called Rajasuya and defeat the powerful king, Jarasandha.

42

Bhima and Jarasandha had a wrestling match in which Bhima killed Jarasandha by breaking him into two pieces and throwing both pieces away from each other.

43

Shishupala the son in law of Jarasandha started cursing Krishna in anger. Krishna forgave him 99 times but the 100th time he used his sudarshan chakra and beheaded Shishupala.
Life lesson: There is a limit to tolerating evil after which you should finish it.

Duryodhana decided to check out the magical palace of Yudhishthira. He accidentally fell into a pond. Draupadi laughed and called him a blind man's son. He swore revenge.

Duryodhana plotted with his evil uncle Shakuni who was a master gambler with dice. He knew Yudhishthira is a poor player but loses control during gambling.

Yudhishthira bet his entire wealth, brothers, himself and even Draupadi and lost. Duryodhana asked Dushashana to drag Draupadi to the court and insulted her in front of everyone.

47

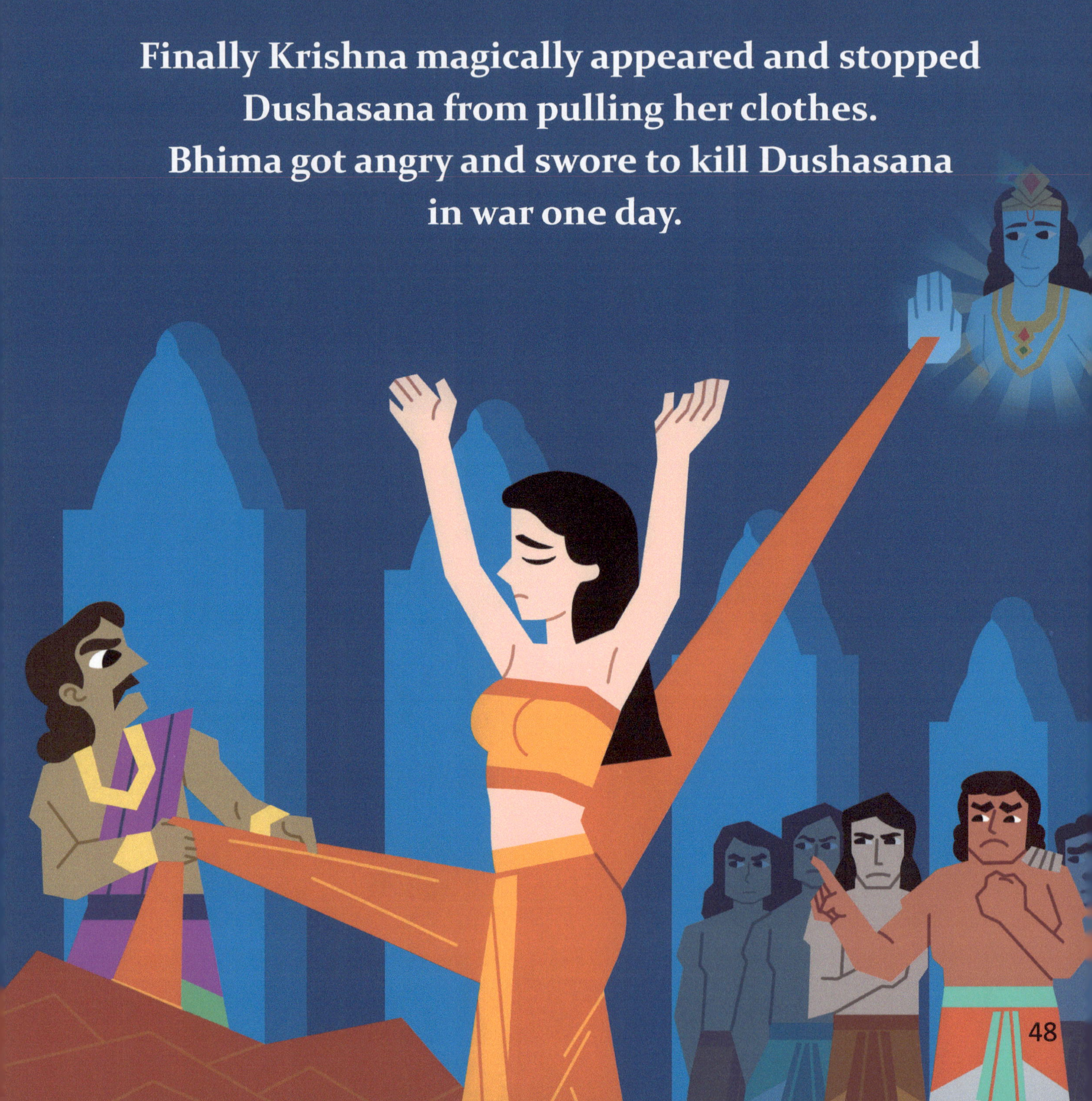
Finally Krishna magically appeared and stopped
Dushasana from pulling her clothes.
Bhima got angry and swore to kill Dushasana
in war one day.
48

Kauravas put a condition that Pandavas will go in exile for twelve years and live one year in disguise. If their disguise is caught, they have to repeat twelve years.

Life lesson: Do not ever gamble blindly.

Pandavas spent their last year in Matsya kingdom.
Bhima disguised as a cook, Arjuna a dancer,
Yudhishthira a gambler, Sahadev a cowherd,
Draupadi a maid and Nakul a stable boy.

50

After exile, Pandavas asked for just five towns but Duryodhana refused. War was inevitable. Krishna knew that with Karna in the opposite camp victory is impossible.

Life lesson: Wars are destructive and should be considered only if negotiations fail.

Arjuna's father, Indra, asked Karna to give away his protective armor (kavach-kundal). Knowing it was a trick, Karna still cut it from his body and gave it, being a daan veer (generous).

Life lesson: People can take advantage of you if you're too generous.

Kunti also went and revealed to Karna that she is his mother. She asked him to join Pandavas. Karna refused but promised her that'll he'll not kill any Pandava except Arjuna.

53

The eighteen day Mahabharat war began.
On day one, Arjuna panicked, refusing to fight his
own kin. Krishna then revealed the secrets of
creation and dharma, known as the Bhagavad Gita.
Life lesson: Do your best and leave the rest to God.

For nine days, intense fighting led to thousands of deaths, but Bhishma protected Hastinapur. That evening, the Pandavas visited Bhishma in his tent, where he revealed the secret to his defeat.

55

The next day, Arjuna placed Shikandi,
a half-woman, half-man, before Bhishma.
Shikandi was the reborn princess Amba, who had
vowed to kill Bhishma after being rejected by
Prince Salva.

Bhishma, bound to not fight unless his opponent was fully male, was targeted by Arjuna, who shot arrows, bringing Bhishma down. Bhishma lay on a bed of arrows until he chose to die.

On the thirteenth day, Dronacharya created the chakravyuh formation. Only Arjuna's son, Abhimanyu, knew how to break in, having learned it in the womb. He didn't know how to exit.

Life lesson: Half knowledge is dangerous.

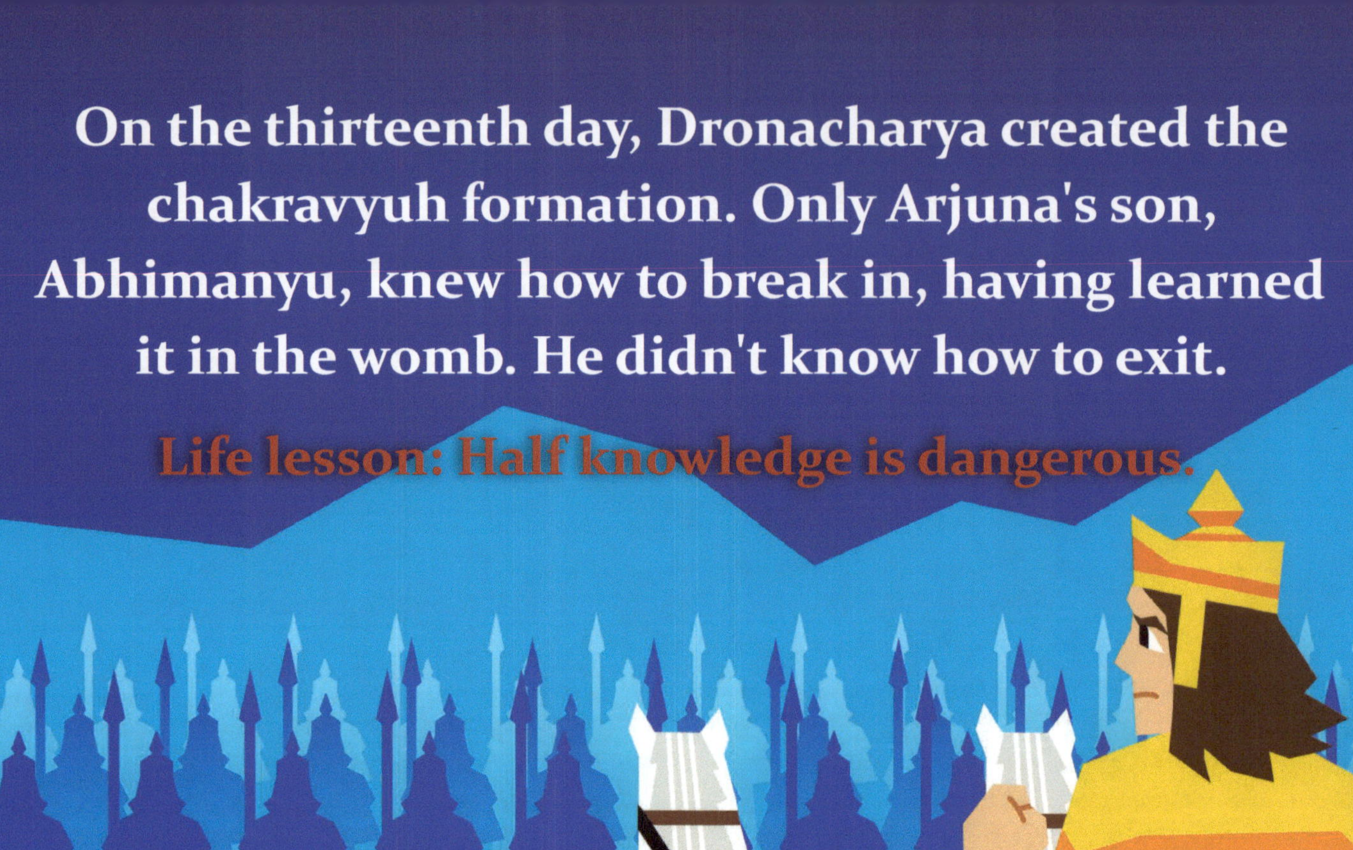

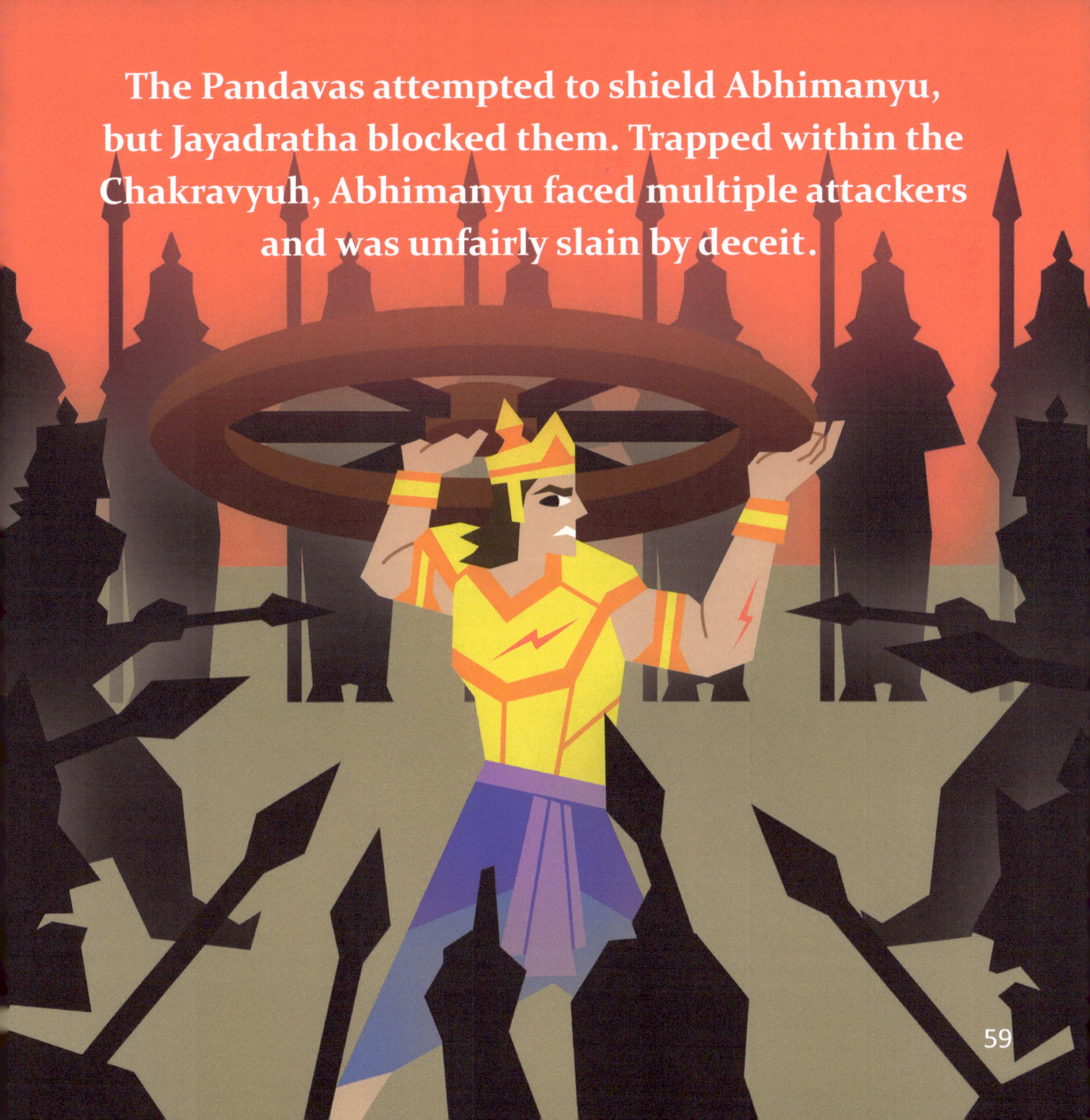

The Pandavas attempted to shield Abhimanyu, but Jayadratha blocked them. Trapped within the Chakravyuh, Abhimanyu faced multiple attackers and was unfairly slain by deceit.

When Arjuna got to know about his son's death he vowed that he'll burn himself to death on a pyre if he is unable to kill Jayadhrath before the next day ends.

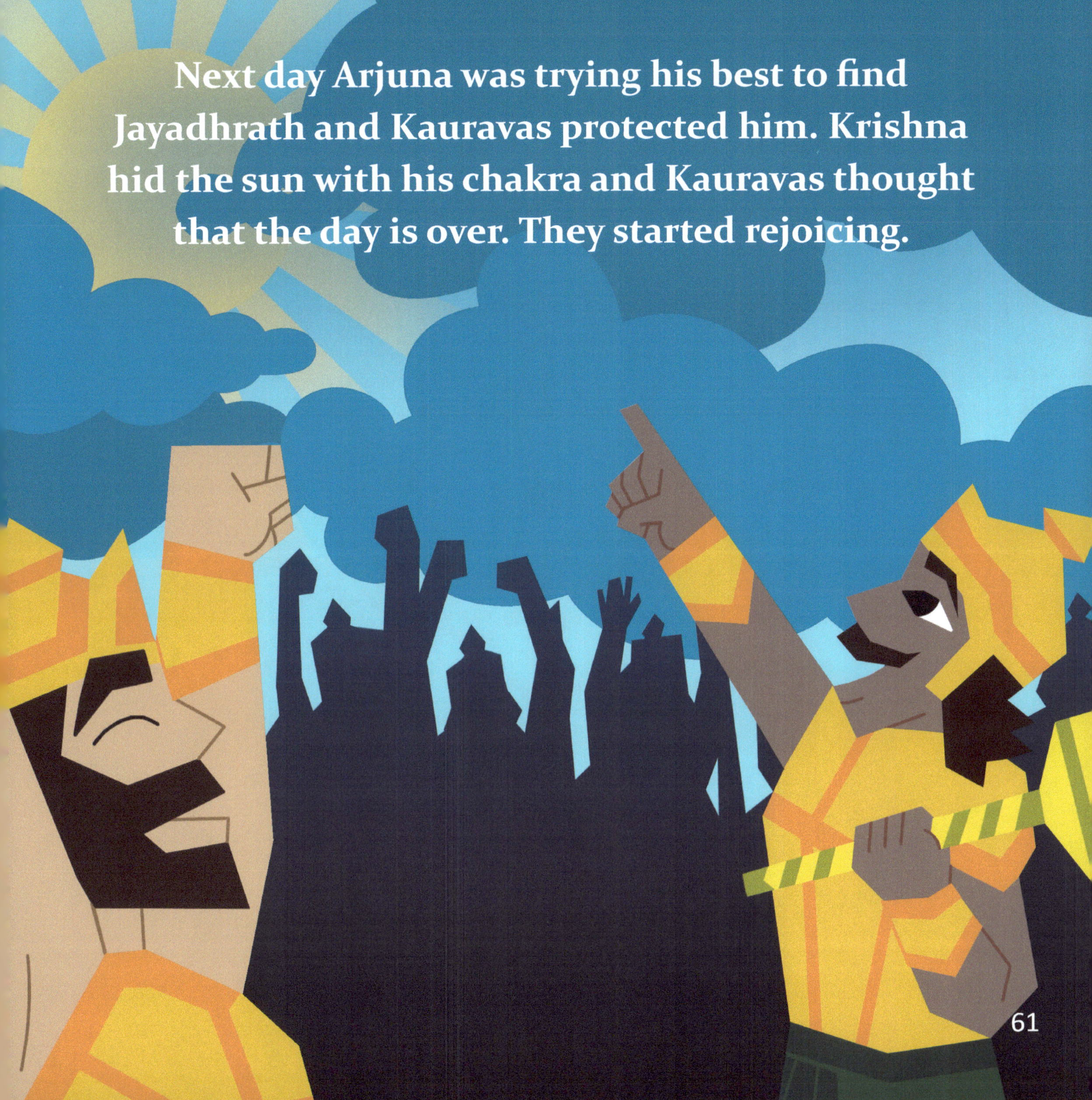

Next day Arjuna was trying his best to find Jayadhrath and Kauravas protected him. Krishna hid the sun with his chakra and Kauravas thought that the day is over. They started rejoicing.

Krishna suddenly released the chakra, revealing it was still daytime. Jayadratha, exposed, was killed by Arjuna's Pashupatiastra.
With Jayadratha gone, the remaining major threat to the Pandavas was Karna.

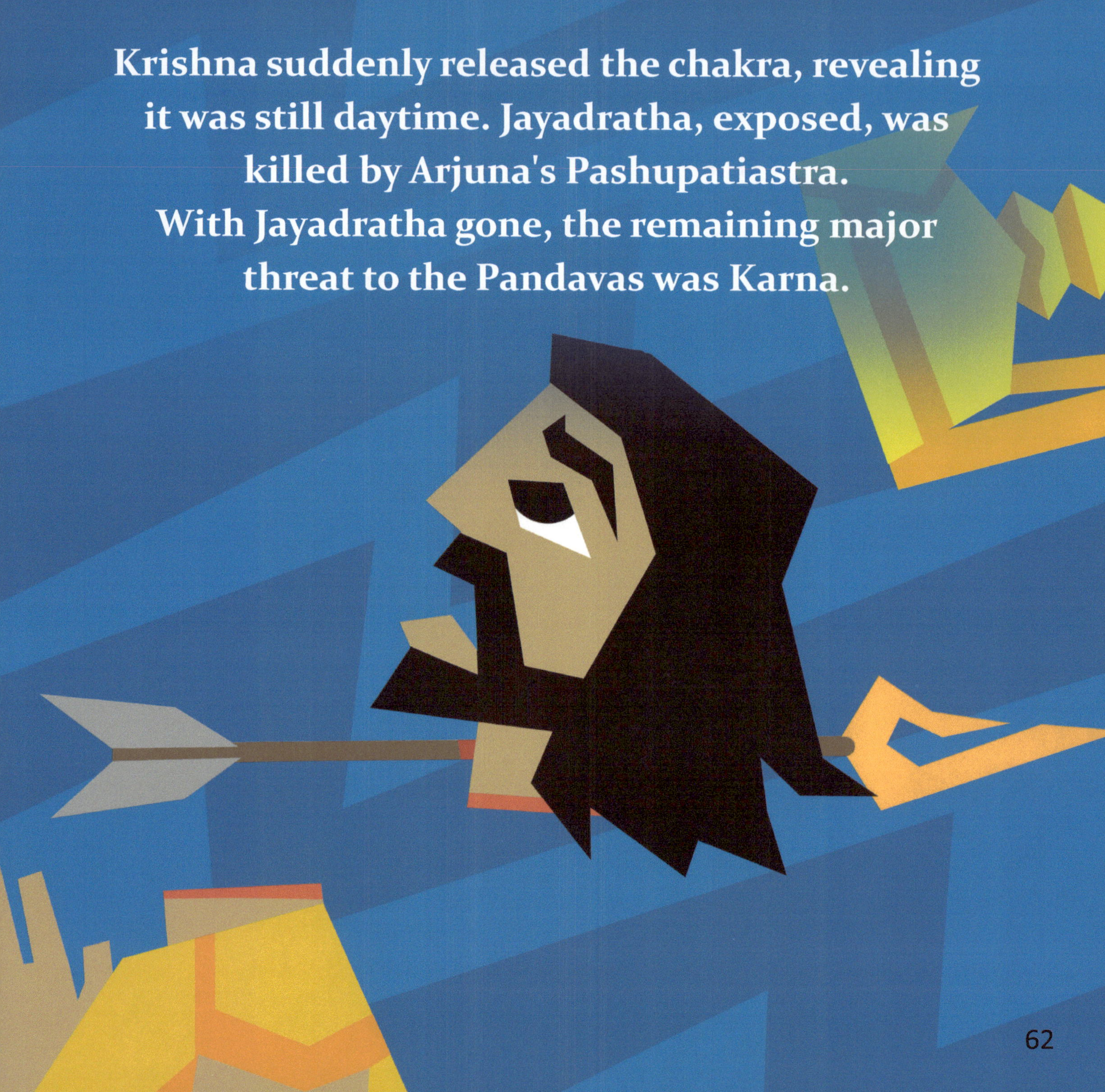

Krishna revealed Karna couldn't be killed while he had the Shakti astra. To neutralize it, Bhima's son Ghatotkach was sent into battle. Overwhelmed by Ghatotkach's destruction, Duryodhana urged Karna to use Shakti.

Karna used the Shakti astra to kill Ghatotkach,
who sacrificed himself for the Pandavas.
With his kavach-kundal gone and Shakti used up,
Karna was vulnerable. Yet, Drona remained a
major threat.

Krishna exploited Drona's weakness—his son, Ashwathamma. Bhima killed an elephant named Ashwathamma and told Drona that Ashwathamma is dead. Drona confirmed with Yudhishthira, who never lied.

For the first time, Yudhishthira told a half-truth, softly adding "the elephant" after saying, "Ashwathamma is dead." Grieving, Drona stopped fighting and sat in meditation. While his eyes were closed, Dhrishtadyumna unfairly killed him.

On day seventeen, Bhima battled Dushasana. After defeating him, Bhima tore Dushasana's chest and drank his blood. Draupadi then washed her hair in his blood, avenging her humiliation.

On the same day, Karna and Arjuna fought fiercely. Karna's chariot wheel got stuck due to a curse. Following Krishna's advice, Arjuna shot Karna, who forgot his defensive mantra from Parshuram's curse, and was killed.

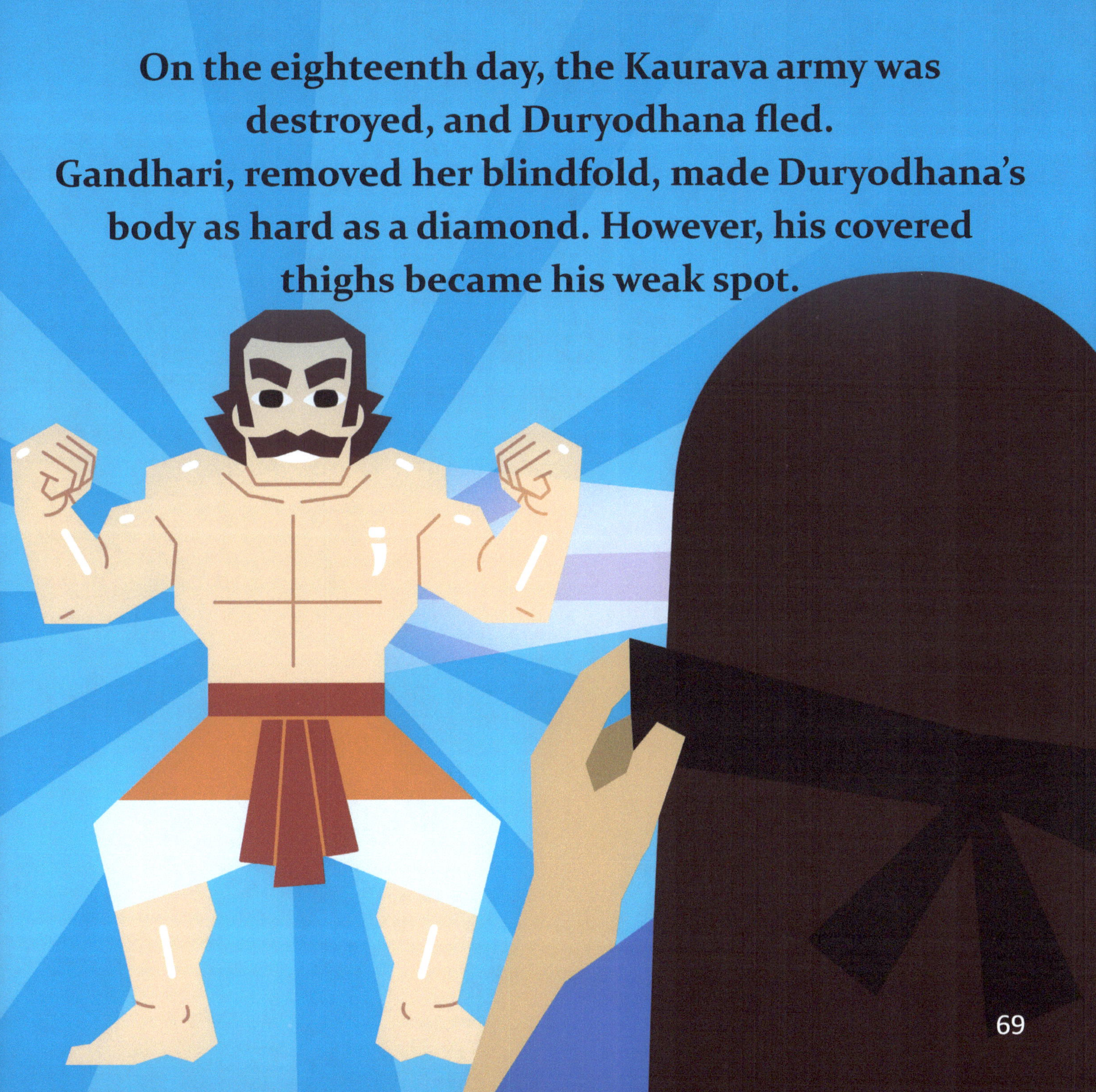

On the eighteenth day, the Kaurava army was destroyed, and Duryodhana fled. Gandhari, removed her blindfold, made Duryodhana's body as hard as a diamond. However, his covered thighs became his weak spot.

During the fight between Bhima and Duryodhana, Krishna told Bhima to strike at Duryodhana´s thighs. Before dying, Duryodhana made Ashwathamma the commander of the Kaurava army and asked him to attack the Pandava camp at night.

Ashwathamma killed all of Draupadi's sleeping sons and targeted a Brahmastra at Uttara's unborn child. Krishna reversed this, saving the child, and cursed Ashwathamma to wander the world in eternal pain, never dying.

Life lesson: Attacking unarmed people and unborn children is the greatest evil.

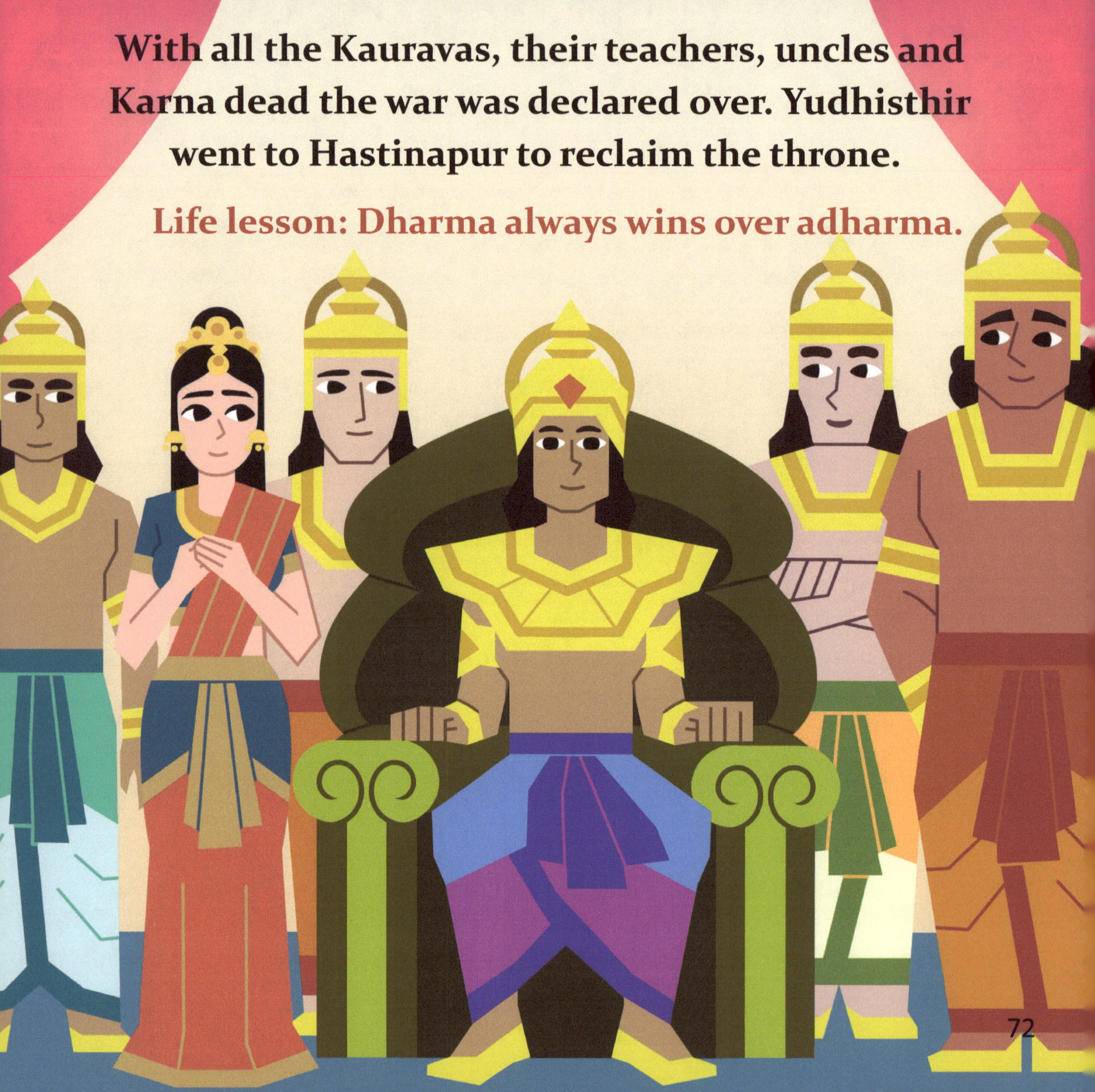

With all the Kauravas, their teachers, uncles and Karna dead the war was declared over. Yudhisthir went to Hastinapur to reclaim the throne.

Life lesson: Dharma always wins over adharma.

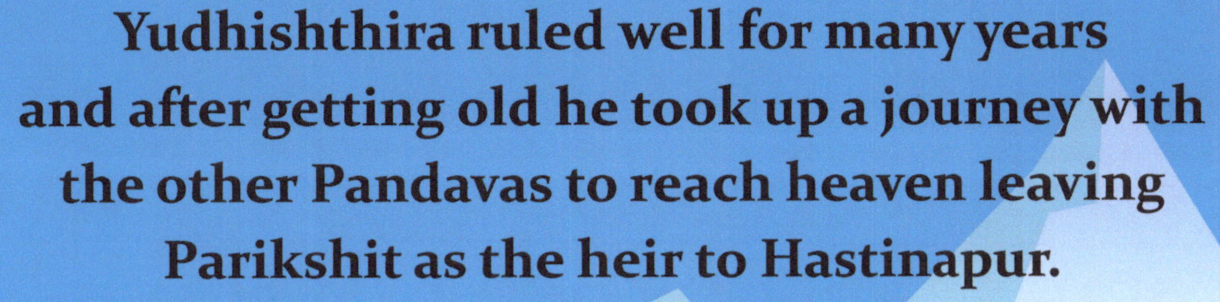

Yudhishthira ruled well for many years
and after getting old he took up a journey with
the other Pandavas to reach heaven leaving
Parikshit as the heir to Hastinapur.

Mahabharata puzzles and quiz

How many children did Shantanu and Ganga have together including Devavrata (Bhishma)?

A) 5 + 4   B) 4 + 3   C) 7 + 1   D) 5 + 1

One out of the three princesses, Amba, Ambika, and Ambalika, did not want to marry Vichitraveerya. How much is one out of three?

A) A quarter **B) A half** **C) A fifth** **D) A third**

Gandhari cannot see as she has tied a blindfold over her eyes. Can you please lead her through the maze to Dhritharashtra's royal chamber?

King Pandu had Pandavas with Queen Kunti and Madri. How many Pandavas were there?

A) 2 multiplied by 3   B) 9 divided by 3

C) 10 divided by 2   D) 3 + 4

Kunti has left baby Karna to float away in the river. Help him navigate to his foster father Adhiratha.

King Dhritharasthra and Queen Gandhari had Kauravas in pots filled with ghee and a piece of Gandhari's flesh. How many Kauravas were there?

A) 90 + 5   B) 107 - 9   C) 93 + 7   D) 105 - 6

Ekalavya has cut a part of his body to pay as a fee to Dronacharya. Choose the correct part from the options below.

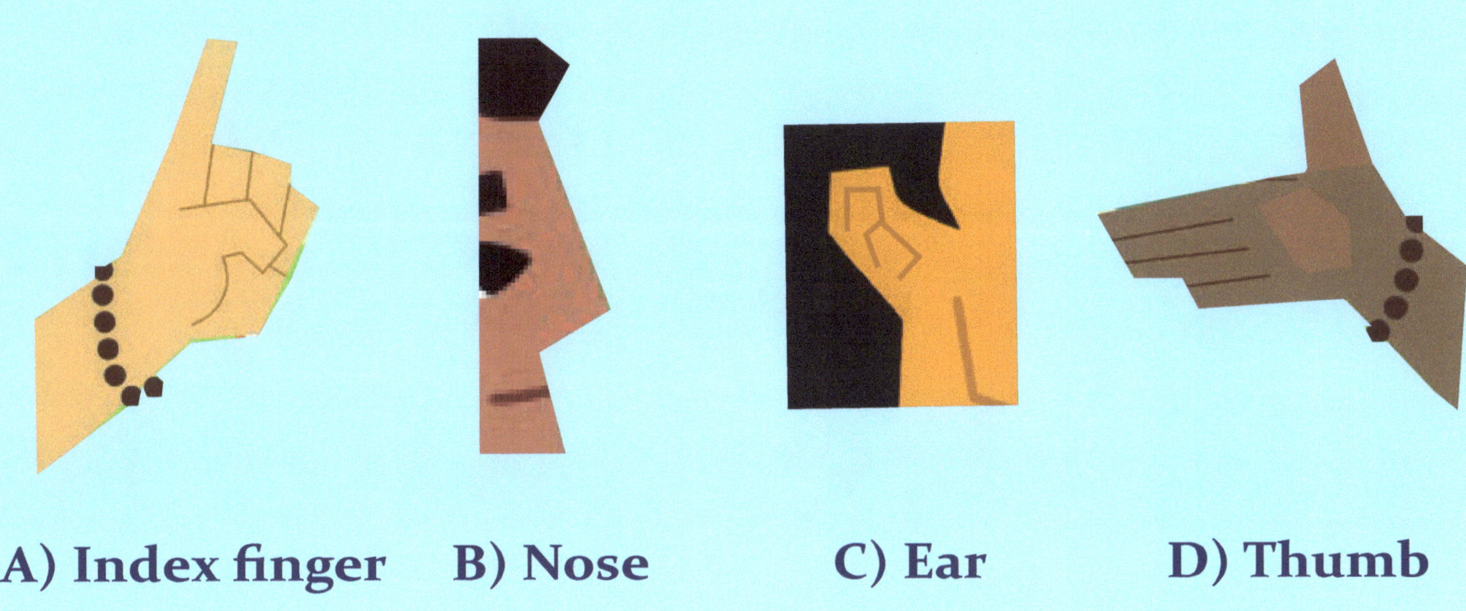

The wheel takes 60 seconds to do a full circle. Arjuna needs 3 seconds to aim and shoot. If the wheel starts now, in how many seconds should Arjuna prepare to aim and shoot?

A) 58 seconds   B) 59 seconds   C) 55 seconds   D) 57 seconds

Draupadi married all five Pandavas based on Kunti's suggestion. So how much of a wife was she to each Pandava?

A) One third B) One fourth C) One fifth D) Half

Shakuni has thrown the dice and this is the number he got. Yudhisthir is next. Pick which number would beat Shakuni.

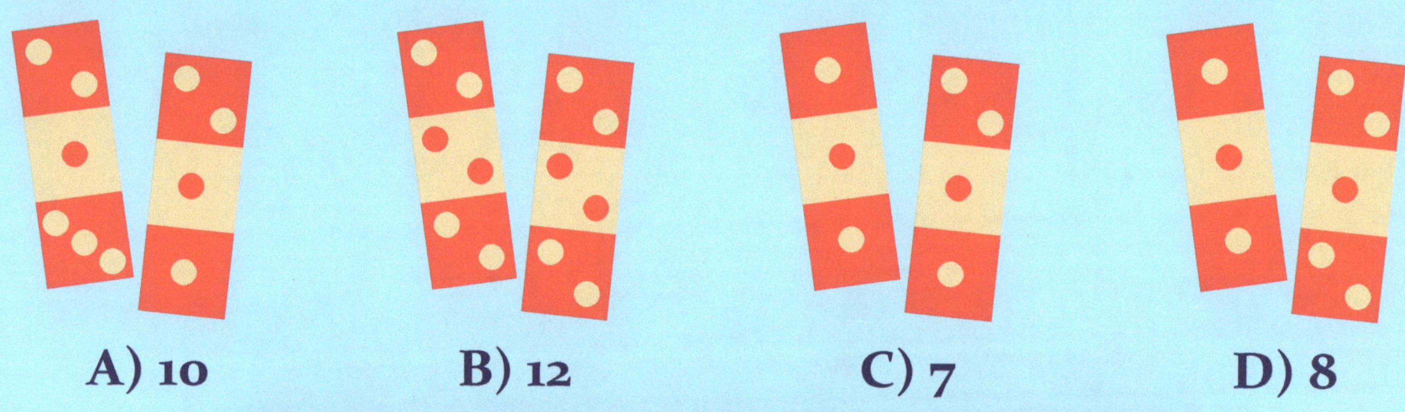

A) 10   B) 12   C) 7   D) 8

Color this picture **of Pandavas sitting sad after being exiled to the forest for twelve years after losing a gambling game with Shakuni and Duryodhan.**

In the one year of agyaatvaas (living in disguise), the Pandavas took up different jobs in king Virat's court. Which one of the following is incorrect?

A) Bheema - Cook   B) Arjuna - Dancer   C) Yudhisthir - Doctor

D) Sahadev– Cow herd   E) Draupadi – Maid   C) Nakul – Stable boy

Color this picture of Shree Krishna showing the Vishwaroopam form to Arjuna during the revelation of Bhagavad Gita.

Each arrow can hold 4 pounds.
Bhishma is 200 pounds.
What are the minimum number of arrows needed to hold Bhishma?

A) 48   B) 49   C) 50   D) 47

Abhimanyu is trapped inside the chakravuyha. Please help him get out of it.

The elephant **Ashwathamma** can endure a force of 10 tons hitting its head. The weight of different parts of Bhima's mace are provided below. Add it up and see if Bheema will be able to strike it dead.

A) 3 tons   B) 1 tons   C) 5 tons   D) 2 tons

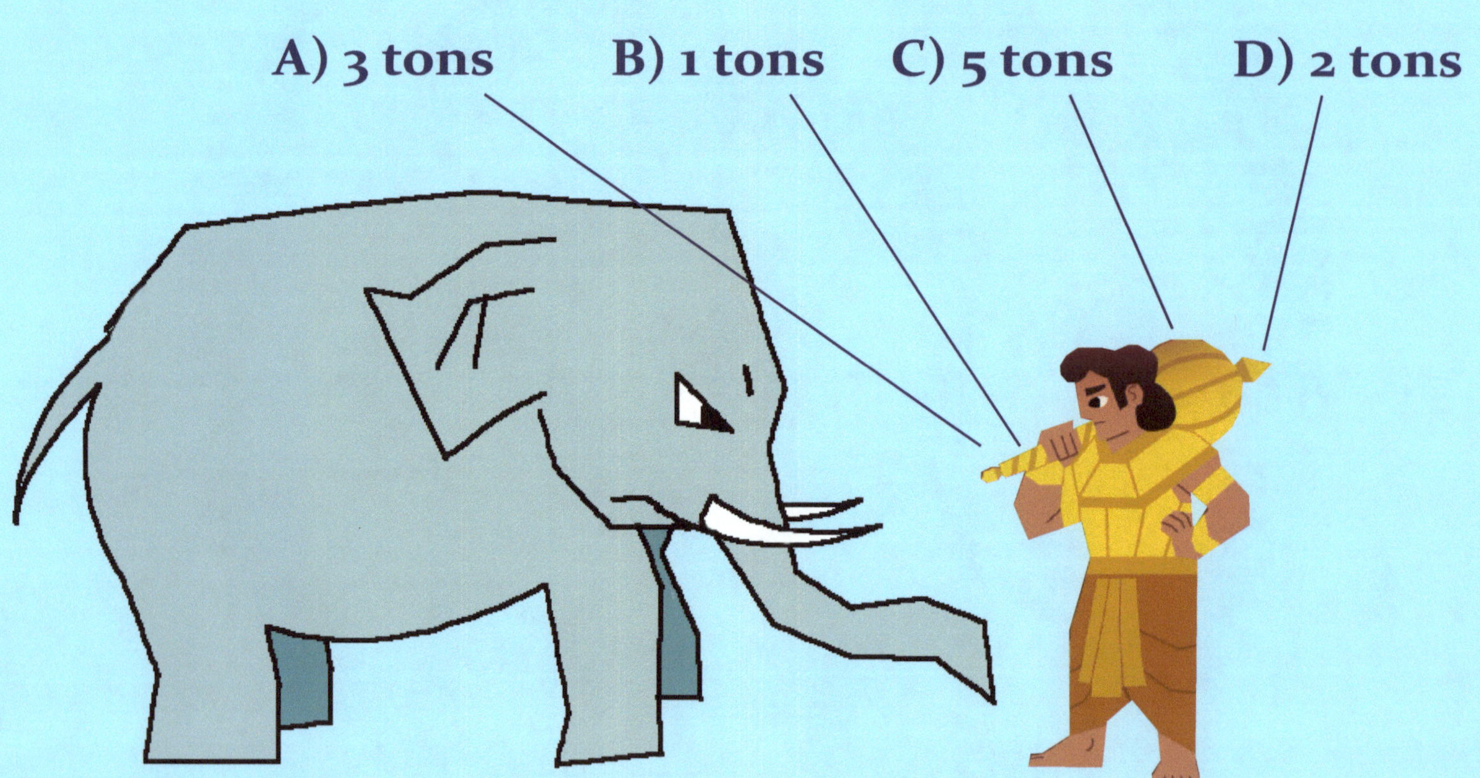

Karna can move 100 kilos with each hand. The wheel is 202 kilos. Will he be able to move it in time before Arjuna shoots the arrow at him?

A) Yes   **B) No**

Color this picture of Pandavas in Hastinapur after winning the Mahabharata war.

Final quiz – Score 15 or more to become a Mahabharat champion

Q1) Which river did King Shantanu fall in love with?
a) Saraswati   b) Ganga   c) Godavari   d) Jamuna

Q2) What name was given to Devavrata after he took a vow to never marry?
a) Grishmaa   b) Sushma   c) Dushmaa   d) Bhishma

Q3) Which one of the following was not one of the princesses married to Vichitraveerya?
a) Amika   b) Amba   c) Ambika   d) Ambalika

Q4) Who was the Rishi who used magical powers to create Dhritharashtra and Pandu?
a) Rishi Kashyap   b) Rishi Vyasa   c) Rishi Valmiki   d) Rishi Bharadwaj

Q5) Who was Dhritharashtra's wife who put a blindfold over her eyes?
a) Gandhari   b) Mandari   c) Sundari   d) Bhandari

Q6) What were the 100 sons of Dhritharashtra and Gandhari born from pots called?
a) Shauravas   b) Dhruvas   c) Kauravas   d) Bhairavas

Q7) What were sons of Pandu with his two wives Kunti and Madri called?
a) Gandavas   b) Pandavas   c) Mandavas   d) Bhandavas

Q8) Who was the son that Kunti secretly had with Surya dev before she got married?
a) Svarna   b) Bharna   c) Marna   d) Karna

Q9) Who was the main teacher for the Kauravas and Pandavas?
a) Drona   b) Aristotle   c) Socrates   d) Mona

Q10) Which princess did Arjuna win in a swayamvar but then became wife of all Pandavas?
a) Shatapati   b) Draupadi   c) Marupudi   d) Didi

Q11) Who cut off his thumb as a fee for Dronacharya?
a) Duskalavya   b) Teenkalavya   c) Ekalavya   d) Chaarkalavya

Q12) Who was Duryodhana's evil uncle that defeated the Pandavas in a dice game and sent them to 14 years of exile?
a) Dushashan   b) Sakya muni   c) Shakuni   d) Sakira

Q13) Who was Duryodhana's brother that pulled Draupadi's clothes after winning the gambling game?
a) Shalya   b) Jayadhrata   c) Dushasana   d) Nakul

Q14) Which God revealed the Gita to Arjuna before the Mahabharat war started?
a) Shiva   b) Brahma   c) Ganesha   d) Krishna

Q15) What was princess Amba reborn as to kill Bhishma?
a) Pakhandi   b) Shikandi   c) Drupad   d) Dhristadhum

Q16) What was the formation in which Arjuna's son Abhimanyu knew how to get in but didn't know how to get out?
a) Sea view   b) Chakravyuh   c) Bhul bhulaiya   d) Maze formation

Q17) Drona's son and an elephant had the same name. What was it?
a) Ashwathamma   b) Gajraj   c) Jumbo   d) Appu

Q18) Who was Bhima's son with demoness Hidimba, who was killed by Karna in the war?
a) Bakasur   b) Jayadhratt   c) Ghatothkach   d) Sahadev

Q19) Which part of the body did Bhima strike and kill Duryodhana?
a) Chest   b) Back   c) Head   d) Thighs

Q20) How many days did the Mahabharat war last?
a) 28 days   b) 10 days   c) 18 days   d) 25 days

Answers

1) B
2) D
3) A
4) B
5) A
6) C
7) B
8) D
9) A
10) B
11) C
12) C
13) C
14) D
15) B
16) B
17) A
18) C
19) D
20) C